MASTERING
PHYSICS

Understanding *the* Laws *of* Thermodynamics

RANDALL McPARTLAND

Cavendish
Square
New York

Published in 2015 by Cavendish Square Publishing, LLC
243 5th Avenue, Suite 136, New York, NY 10016

Copyright © 2015 by Cavendish Square Publishing, LLC

First Edition

Website: cavendishsq.com

This publication represents the opinions and views of the author based on his or her personal experience, knowledge, and research. The information in this book serves as a general guide only. The author and publisher have used their best efforts in preparing this book and disclaim liability rising directly or indirectly from the use and application of this book.

CPSIA Compliance Information: Batch #WW15CSQ

All websites were available and accurate when this book was sent to press.

Library of Congress Cataloging-in-Publication Data

McPartland, Randall.
Understanding the laws of thermodynamics / by Randall McPartland.
p. cm. — (Mastering physics)
Includes index.
ISBN 978-1-50260-135-3 (hardcover) ISBN 978-1-50260-133-9 (ebook)
1. Thermodynamics — Juvenile literature. I. Title.
QC311.M73 2015
536—d23

Senior Editor: Fletcher Doyle
Senior Copy Editor: Wendy A. Reynolds
Art Director: Jeffrey Talbot
Senior Designer: Amy Greenan
Senior Production Manager: Jennifer Ryder-Talbot
Production Editor: David McNamara
Photo Research by J8 Media

The photographs in this book are used by permission and through the courtesy of: Cover photo and page 1, Ryan McVay/Stone/Getty Images; bogdanhoda/Shutterstock.com, 5; prudkov/Shutterstock.com, 6; Zurijeta/Shutterstock.com, 8; Gavran333/Shutterstock.com, 9; Andersen Ross/Blend Images/Getty Images, 11; prognone/iStock/Thinkstock, 14; Dean Pennala/Shutterstock.com, 16; Barry Skeetes/File:Marshall Sons Traction Engine "Old Timer?", Gloucestershire Steam & Vintage Extravaganza 2013.jpg/Wikimedia Commons, 19; Rainer Schlegelmilch/Getty Images, 21; Kat Miner/File:San Diego skyline against smoke from wildfires Oct 2007/Wikimedia Commons, 22; Jorge Royan/File:Berlin- An electricity power plant smokestack in - 3982/Wikimedia Commons, 25; Sean Gallup/Getty Image News/Getty Images, 26 (top); Timothy A. Clary/AFP/Getty Images, 26 (bottom); File:Carnot cycle p-V diagram/Wikimedia Commons, 28; Joe Belanger/Shutterstock.com, 30; JoeyPhoto/Shutterstock.com, 31; Yuri Arcurs/Hemera/Thinkstock, 32; cynoclub/iStock/Thinkstock, 35; nano/E+/Getty Images, 36; vuttichai chaiya/Shutterstock.com, 38; Hurst Photo/Shutterstock.com, 39; Solar Roadways, 40; Smithsonian Institution/File:Walther Nernst SI/Wikimedia Commons, 43.

Printed in the United States of America

CONTENTS

INTRODUCTION

G lobal warming is a growing concern. Reducing it is just one area in which **thermodynamics** can play an important role. The laws of thermodynamics deal with transformations of energy. The word is derived from two Greek words: *therm*, or **heat**, and *dynamis*, or **force**. **Work** is another word for force.

Most work used to be done by humans. Now, we use heat to generate, or make, the electricity to do work for us. Electricity is mostly generated by burning fossil fuels, such as coal, oil, and gas. The creation of electricity is a transformation of energy. Therefore, it is an illustration of the first law of thermodynamics, or the law of conservation of energy. This says that energy can be neither created nor destroyed, although it can be transferred from one form to another. It also says that after the fossil fuels are burned, there is the same amount of energy present.

There is a **finite** amount of fossil fuels available. Remember the first law. We can't create energy. The energy for those fuels comes from the sun, and the process to create them takes a long time.

There have been many statements of the second law. One is that when heat is transformed into work, some heat must be discarded, or let go. Another is that heat can flow only from a hotter object to a cooler object.

Burning fossil fuels creates gases that block the escape of increasing amounts of heat from our atmosphere. Heat flows from the sun to the cooler earth during the day. Some of this heat is reflected into our atmosphere. At night, the heat reverses course and

Energy, not muscle, now does most of our heavy lifting.

heads to the cooler air. Since more of this heat doesn't escape our atmosphere, our climate is getting warmer.

The third law deals with the behavior of a property called entropy, which is a measure of the tendency of energy to move outward from a concentrated area. The zeroth law clarifies the definition of temperature.

Thermodynamics is important in engineering and many branches of science. It is being used to find ways to transfer the sun's energy into electricity in a way that won't create greenhouse gases so we can do the work we need to do without baking ourselves.

A woman who weighs 130 pounds (58.9 kg) has to work for thirty minutes at a speed of 3 miles per hour (4.8 kmh) to burn off ninety-two calories on a treadmill.

ONE

Writing a New Law

You have likely heard of **calories** in terms of food and how much energy the food you eat provides your body. The word calorie actually comes from a mistaken theory about the nature of heat and energy. Scientists in the eighteenth century believed that heat was an invisible fluid called "caloric." Although theories on caloric were disproved, scientists kept the word "calorie" as one of the units of heat, and we still use phrases such as "flow of heat."

The first law of thermodynamics states that energy can neither be created from nothing, nor destroyed. For every physical process in which energy is transferred, whether it is boiling water or turning a waterwheel, the total amount of energy involved never changes.

In formulating the first law, scientists redefined the concept of energy. They realized that heat and work were two different ways of transferring energy, and that each could be converted into the other. We take this for granted. Coal or gas burned at power plants produces heat, which in turn provides the energy that runs our computers and hair dryers. For scientists of centuries past, though, discoveries about the nature of energy changed physics and engineering completely.

It takes a lot of work to move materials from ground level to a rooftop bricklayer.

WORKING WITHIN A SYSTEM

Thermodynamic analyses often focus on processes within an area of interest, called a **system**. A thermodynamic system is defined by its **boundary**, which separates it from its surroundings. A system can be a glass of water, or an amount of gas in an airtight cylinder. Some systems may interact with their surroundings. An isolated system is one that does not exchange heat or work across the boundary.

Experiments showed that heat was not a substance as scientists once thought. Instead, it was a method of transferring energy. Basically, energy is the ability to make something move. The field of thermodynamics distinguishes between two methods of transferring

A snug-fitting lid can make the inside your coffee mug approximate a closed system.

energy, which are work and heat.

Work is a force that acts through **displacement**, which refers to an object's change in position. If someone is fixing a chimney, for example, they have to move the new bricks from the ground to the roof. Lifting the weight of these bricks, either manually or mechanically, and moving them is work.

Heat, as defined in thermodynamics, is the transference of energy across the boundary of one system to another system at a lower temperature because of a difference in temperature between the two systems. No work can be done if the systems are at the same temperature. So, heat is the transference of energy resulting from the interaction of a hot and a cold object.

If you add an ice cube to a cup of coffee, heat will be transferred from the coffee to the ice cube (hotter to colder). The ice will melt, and the mixture of coffee and water will reach the same temperature. This state is called **thermal equilibrium**. The temperature of the coffee will cool further because the air around it is cooler and the coffee, which is not in a closed system, will interact with its surroundings. It will release heat into the air until it reaches room temperature.

In thermodynamic terms, once the coffee mix hits room temperature it no longer contains heat, since there is no longer any transfer of energy from one system to another. Putting coffee into an

Calorie Counter

C alorie is a commonly used word but you must be careful to use it correctly. There are many kinds of calories.

The one most of us use refers to the amount of energy we get from food. This energy can be obtained from different sources, such as carbohydrates, fats, and proteins. All of these provide the energy we need to live. These calories are, in fact, kilocalories, which are large calories.

The original calorie was defined as the heat needed at a pressure of one standard atmosphere to raise the temperature of one gram of water 1 degree Celsius. Equal to about 4.2 **joules**, this has been called a small calorie.

The calorie in food is one thousand of the original calories. This means that cup of yogurt you think is only 120 calories is really 120,000 original calories. Thinking of it that way might ruin your appetite.

The energy in food is measured in calories—which can turn into extra pounds.

insolated mug with a good lid approximates a closed system because it restricts the ability of the hot liquid and the cool air to interact.

Temperature is a measure of how hot or cold something is. Long after the formulation of the first and second laws of thermodynamics, scientists were frustrated by the lack of a precise definition of temperature. In 1931, R. H. Fowler proposed the "zeroth law of thermodynamics" as a solution. It states that if two systems are in thermal equilibrium with a third system, the two systems will be in thermal equilibrium with each other. For example, if a thermometer inserted in a **beaker** of water reads 25 degrees Celsius, and a second beaker of water is also measured at 25 degrees Celsius, the two beakers of water are at thermal equilibrium.

This concept is crucial to temperature measurement in thermodynamics. The zeroth law is an observation that allows us to make a thermometer. When liquids get hotter, they expand. A thermometer allows us to assign a temperature to a system it comes in contact with by how much the liquid inside it expands.

We calibrate the change in a thermal property, which we can observe because of the marks on the thermometer, by putting the thermometer in thermal equilibrium with a known physical system at several reference points. Celsius thermometers have the reference points fixed at the freezing and boiling point of pure water and assign those points zero and one hundred degrees. If we bring the thermometer into thermal equilibrium with any other system, we can now determine the temperature of the other system.

CANNON LAW

Two men provided the proof that led to the demise of the caloric theory and the formulation of the first law of thermodynamics.

In 1797, the physicist Benjamin Thompson, otherwise known as Count Rumford, was overseeing the manufacture of cannons. As an experiment, he bored the barrel of a cannon immersed in water with a dull drill bit turned by horses. Friction from the drill bit grinding the barrel produced heat. After two and a half hours, onlookers were astonished to see that the water was boiling without being heated by a fire.

Rumford believed that he had proven that motion produced heat and that heat was not a substance called "caloric." As he did not take measurements he could not quantitatively connect motion and heat, so other scientists were not convinced.

Scientist James Joule made the connection in the 1840s by making precise measurements during his experiments. He began with experiments on **electromagnets** and electric current. Joule devised an apparatus where a pair of weights passing over pulleys performed work that generated an electric current. The current produced heat. Joule could calculate the amount of heat produced by the work, a figure he called the "mechanical equivalent of heat."

Joule attached a thermometer to a paddle wheel immersed in water. The paddle wheel was turned by a descending weight. Joule was able to measure precisely the work done by the weight and the resulting temperature increase of the water.

Rumford and Joule both demonstrated that work could be converted into heat. Joule proved that a fixed amount of work—in this case the descending weight—is required to generate one unit of heat. Energy, not heat, is conserved during the transformation. This conclusion refuted the caloric theory of heat, which assumed that heat itself was conserved in the form of "caloric." Joule's work became the foundation of the first law of thermodynamics.

Joule measured mechanical work in **foot–pounds**, while heat was measured in **BTU**, or **British thermal units**. A foot-pound is a unit of work equal to the work done by a force of one pound acting through a distance of one foot in the direction of the force. He calculated that 772 foot-pounds of work would produce one BTU. Today, we know that the actual figure for the mechanical equivalent of heat is 778.26 foot-pounds per BTU. Scientists use the joule, abbreviated J, as the unit for measuring energy, work, and heat. One joule equals 0.239 calories.

APPLYING THE FIRST LAW

The first law of thermodynamics leads to a number of corollaries, or consequences. The most important is that any change in the internal energy of a system is equal to the difference between the

Computer controlled heliostats keep reflected sunlight concentrated on a target.

Understanding the Laws *of* Thermodynamics

heat absorbed by the system and the work done by the system on its surroundings. Internal energy is the energy present in a system when it is stationary, and it exists independent of the motion of the system. According to the first law, if a system performs work, its internal energy will decrease.

If the system absorbs heat, its internal energy will increase. Work can be performed *on* the system and heat transferred *out* of the system. In some cases, work is performed and heat is transferred, but there is no change in the internal energy of the system. This is called a cyclic process. For example, when the weight turned Joule's paddle wheel, it caused heat to be transferred out of the system. The amount of energy transferred by heat equals the amount of energy transferred by work. Cyclic processes are very important in explaining heat engines, or devices that convert heat into mechanical work.

Here is an example of how scientists are using solar energy to operate heat engines. We know that if we put tea bags in a glass container filled with water and set the container in the sun, the water will warm up enough to make tea. However, the heat of the sun is not strong enough to make the water boil, so it takes a long time to make tea this way.

Scientists now place solar reflectors in a field and concentrate the reflection on a central solar power tower. This concentrated solar power is strong enough to boil a liquid inside the tower. This is used to generate electricity in the same way as it is in coal-fired power plants. Heat is transferred out of the system when steam is released to turn the power turbines. The receptors follow the daytime sun to continuously supply a source of heat into the system.

Frozen lakes transfer heat if the air passing over them is frigid.

TWO

The Flow of Heat

et's return to the cup of coffee that has been sitting out and is now cool. We know that in order to reheat it, we have to do something to it.

We know that a mug of hot coffee will naturally cool. Heat is transferred from the coffee to its surroundings. What law of nature prevents the coffee from instead drawing heat from the surroundings?

After all, all things can have heat. In cold climates, frigid winter air causes lakes to freeze. The water in these lakes can never get colder than the freezing point, which is 0 degrees Celsius and 32 degrees Fahrenheit. Therefore, when really cold air, let's say 0 degrees Fahrenheit, passes over a frozen lake, it will increase in temperature.

Why can't heat, then, flow from the air into the coffee? Why can't the coffee spontaneously grow hotter and boil, rather than cooling?

The first law of thermodynamics does not address the direction of heat transfer. The second law of thermodynamics addresses the distribution of heat and energy. One of its statements is that heat naturally flows only from a hot object into a cooler object.

The second law of thermodynamics also has a profound practical impact on the theory and design of heat engines. A car engine burns gasoline to produce heat. The heat is transformed into the mechanical energy that runs the car. According to the second law, the engine cannot have 100 percent efficiency, because it is impossible for all of the heat to be transformed into mechanical energy.

In the car, only 14 to 30 percent of the energy from the burning gasoline is used to move the vehicle. Most of the energy from the gasoline is turned into heat, some of which escapes through an exhaust system. The rest warms the engine.

These engines operate best at around 200 degrees F (93 degrees C) but the materials break down if they get a lot hotter. So, some of the energy generated by the burning gas is used to power a water pump. This moves water mixed with liquids that boil at much higher temperatures through passageways in the engine. Heat moves from the engine into the liquid, which then is pumped into the radiator. In the radiator, heat is transferred from the liquid to the air around it, lowering the temperature of the liquid enough so it can be used again to cool the engine.

Finally, the second law addresses entropy, or unavailable energy within a system. In thermodynamic terms, the tendency toward a greater degree of energy dispersal is called an increase in entropy. Scientists can quantify entropy and use an understanding of entropy to predict the behavior of objects in thermodynamic systems.

According to the second law, any spontaneous process in an isolated system will lead to an increase in the entropy of the system. In the case of your car, the burning of gas creates waste heat that, once it is dispersed, goes into a high state of entropy. In this state it would take more energy to recover it than you would get from recycling it.

PERFECT ENGINE

The second law of thermodynamics will forever be associated with Sadi Carnot (1796-1832), a French military engineer who dedicated his short life to studying the steam engine. In 1824, Carnot

Old steam engines operated at about 6 percent efficiency.

published a short book called *Reflections on the Motive Power of Heat and on Machines Appropriate for Developing This Power*. He described a theoretical engine, now called a Carnot engine, that operated at the ideal efficiency. Due to friction and other factors that cause engines to lose energy, no real engine can operate as efficiently as the Carnot engine.

Carnot was the first scientist to understand the potential of the cyclic process in creating an efficient engine. His engine operated in an ideal reversible cycle called the Carnot cycle. During Carnot's day, steam engines operated at only about a 6 percent efficiency, meaning 94 percent of the coal burned to fuel the engine was wasted.

Some engineers tried to improve efficiency by limiting heat loss in engines. Carnot took a different approach. He realized that it was impossible to transform heat into work without discarding some heat. Carnot viewed the engine as having two outlets: one for work, and one for leftover heat. Heat in his engine flowed from a hot source to a cold sink.

RESTATING THE LAW

William Thomson, usually called Lord Kelvin, formulated one statement of the second law. According to the Kelvin statement, no process is possible in which the sole result is the absorption of heat from a reservoir and its complete conversion into work. In other words, when heat is converted into work, some will be lost.

Physicist Rudolph Clausius formulated another statement of the second law in a **monograph**. It was titled, "On the Motive Power of Heat and the Laws Which Can Be Deduced from It for the Theory of Heat." Published in 1850, the paper defined both the first and second laws, and marked the creation of the science of thermodynamics.

According to the Clausius statement of the second law, no process is possible in which the sole result is the transfer of energy from a cooler to a hotter body. Heat flows naturally from hot to cold areas, but not the reverse.

The Clausius statement rules out the possibility of spontaneous refrigeration. A freezer that could run with no need of energy from electricity can't be invented because this would violate the laws of thermodynamics.

Clausius also invented the term "entropy," based on the Greek word for "transformation." During his studies in the new field of

A lot of the heat generated by an automobile engine escapes through the exhaust system.

thermodynamics, he focused on a certain mathematical ratio: heat over temperature. Mathematically, it is written "Q/t," since "Q" is the symbol used for heat in thermodynamic equations. The ratio represents the amount of heat transferred and the temperature, before and after the heat transfer.

Clausius examined the ratio for different kinds of processes involving heat transfer, beginning with the heat transferred in a

Heat Death

San Diego is often described as having the perfect climate. In this idealized view, often held by people who live in cold and snowy places, the temperature range in that California city is small, never too hot and never too cold. While this sounds lovely, it can be used as a description of the death of the universe.

Heat Death is just a theory, and it will happen only if the universe lasts nearly an infinite amount of time. The theory is that if all available energy has been transferred from a hot source to a cold source, then the universe will reach a state of thermal equilibrium. We are doing some of this with thermal pollution and the release of heat through the burning of fossil fuels, which increases the entropy of the universe.

If thermal equilibrium happens, no work can be extracted from the universe because there are no temperature differences to create work, so for human purposes, the universe is dead. The world will have reached maximum entropy, and humankind will not be able to restore order.

Smoke from wildfires in 2007 is illuminated at dawn in San Diego.

reversible engine. The ratio stayed constant for a reversible cycle. Clausius went on to examine irreversible processes, such as heat being transferred from a hot cup of coffee. Q/t increased for such processes. Clausius renamed the Q/t ratio, calling it entropy. Unlike energy, entropy is not conserved during natural processes. Clausius concluded that the entropy of the universe naturally tends to increase.

THERMAL POLLUTION

For years, environmentalists have attacked air pollution emitted by fossil fuel-burning power plants. Most people are unaware of another by-product of these plants, thermal pollution. As shown by the second law, it is impossible to convert all of the heat generated in a power plant into mechanical energy. Waste heat is released into the environment.

Power plants burn fossil fuels to produce heat, which converts water into steam. At this point, about 12 percent of the energy is lost in the chimney stack. The steam passes through a turbine that generates electrical power from the steam. The leftover steam, which is now waste heat, is transferred into a condenser. It condenses into water, which is usually released into a river, pond, or lake.

According to mathematical equations based on the second law, fossil fuel power plants can have a maximum efficiency of only about 66 percent. In reality, power plants generally have an

Understanding the Laws *of* Thermodynamics

Steam escaping through chimneys is waste heat, which is an example of entropy.

overall efficiency of about 40 percent. About 60 percent of all heat generated is released into the environment.

This has an environmental impact all its own. Increases in water temperature can kill fish. Also, hotter water carries less oxygen than cooler water, so a change in water temperature can alter the plant life in a pond, lake, or river.

Increased engine efficiency allows this diesel hybrid by Volkswagen to get 261 miles per gallon (111 kilometers per litre).

THREE

Hot to Cold

esearch shows that we can improve the fuel economy in our cars by up to 50 percent by increasing the efficiency of the engines. As stated earlier, about 70 percent of the heat generated by our internal combustion engines is lost and discarded into our atmosphere.

Carnot dreamed of creating a maximum efficiency engine, an ambition shared by engineers today. He used thermodynamic concepts to solve practical engineering issues. His engine operates in an ideal, reversible cycle, between a high and a low temperature reservoir. The efficiency of the engine depends on the temperatures of the hot and cold reservoirs. One only needs to know the two temperatures to calculate the efficiency. The mathematical term for this quantity is the Carnot efficiency, or the Carnot factor.

INSIDE THE CARNOT ENGINE

An understanding of the Carnot engine requires some basic knowledge of gases. When a gas is compressed into a smaller volume

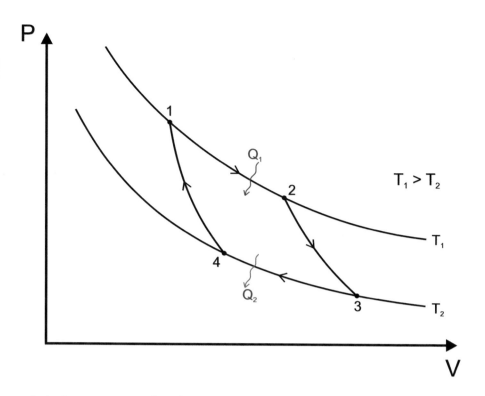

P

Q$_1$

1

2

T$_1$ > T$_2$

T$_1$

4

Q$_2$

3

T$_2$

V

As the Carnot engine goes through its cycle, heat is applied in the first step (Q$_1$) and heat is removed in the third step (Q$_2$). The symbol "T" stands for temperature.

container, such as by a piston, its pressure increases. The pressure of a gas also increases with temperature.

If a gas is kept in contact with a heat source while it is compressed, its temperature will not change. This is called an isothermal compression. The heat source is usually called a heat reservoir. For example, a reservoir could be a water bath that remains at a constant temperature. If there are no heat interactions when the gas is compressed, the temperature of the gas increases. This is called an adiabatic compression.

In a Carnot engine, a quantity of gas is contained in a cylinder fitted with a piston. It exchanges heat with two reservoirs, one at a high temperature and one at a low temperature. The Carnot cycle consists of four reversible processes, two isothermal and two adiabatic.

During the first step at left, the gas is put into contact with the high temperature reservoir (Q_1). The gas absorbs heat from the reservoir and expands in volume. This is an isothermal expansion, since the temperature of the gas is constant. This step produces work by raising the piston.

The second step is an adiabatic expansion. The high temperature reservoir is removed and replaced by an **insulator**. The gas expands adiabatically as pressure and temperature fall. This step also produces work by raising the piston.

No further work can be done by the gas beyond this point, so the gas must be returned to its initial condition. When the gas is cool, it is put on the low temperature reservoir (Q_2) for the third step, an isothermal compression. The piston begins to compress the gas back to its original volume. The gas heats as it is compressed, but the low temperature reservoir absorbs the extra heat. This step consumes work since the piston performs work on the gas.

The fourth step is an adiabatic compression. The low temperature reservoir is removed and replaced by an insulator. The piston continues to compress the gas until it has returned to its original temperature and pressure. This step also consumes work. The gas has returned to its initial conditions, and the cycle can begin again.

The Carnot cycle serves as an example of the statement of the second law dictating that not all heat can be converted into work. An engine operating on a cycle must have a low temperature reservoir, and some heat must be discarded into that reservoir. In an automobile, for example, extra heat is discarded through the radiator and exhaust pipe.

MAXIMIZING ENGINE EFFICIENCY

At first glance, the steps of the Carnot cycle may seem to cancel each other out. The gas produces work during the first two steps, but the last two steps both consume work. How does the engine produce net work?

The efficiency of automobile engines is limited because of the problem of overheating.

The answer lies in the nature of gas. Less work is required to compress gas when it is cool. In the Carnot engine, gas is cooled before it is compressed by the piston. The net work produced depends on the difference between the temperatures of the high and low temperature reservoirs. Therefore, the greater the temperature difference between the two reservoirs, the greater the amount of work produced.

The ratio of the work produced to the heat absorbed is the efficiency of the cycle. Carnot showed that the efficiency depends only on the temperature of the two reservoirs:

$$ec = \frac{TH - TL}{TH}$$

In this equation, "ec" is the efficiency of the Carnot engine. "TH" and "TL" are the temperatures, measured in Kelvin, of the high and low temperature reservoirs. No real engine operating in the cycle between the temperatures TH and TL can be more efficient than the theoretical Carnot engine.

It might seem that to maximize efficiency, the best solution would be to maximize the difference between the two temperatures. In reality, making the high temperature reservoir too hot could damage engine components. The low temperature reservoir is usually around room temperature.

IN AN IDEAL WORLD

Carnot's theoretical engine includes an ideal, reversible cycle that is impossible in the real world. A reversible process is one that, when completed, has returned exactly to its initial conditions. There are no processes in the natural world that are truly reversible.

An ice cube left in a glass on a warm day will melt and will never re-form. Components in a real engine, unlike in the Carnot engine, lose energy through friction.

Once ice melts, it can never re-form.

HEAT PUMPS

Carnot speculated that his engine could operate backward. Rather than transfer heat from a high temperature reservoir to a low temperature reservoir, it would do the opposite. It would remove heat from a low temperature reservoir. According to the second law of thermodynamics, such a process could not be spontaneous.

Heat Exchange

S tanding in front of an open refrigerator might provide momentary relief from the heat but it won't cool the room because the refrigerator moves the heat from one part of the room to another. Two laws of thermodynamics can explain this. The first is that energy moves from a warmer area to a cooler area.

When you put food in a refrigerator, you are trying to remove the heat from it so it will last longer. When a liquid evaporates, it absorbs heat, so to get rid of heat you must convert a liquid to its gaseous state. There are coils on the inside and outside of your refrigerator that carry a refrigerant that boils and turns to gas at close to –15.9 degrees F (–26.6 °C). This refrigerant flows through an expansion valve as the coils enter the refrigerator; as it expands it cools and turns to gas. This absorbs the heat inside the unit.

Another law of thermodynamics is that energy is never destroyed. The heat is not gone; it needs to be dropped off somewhere else. To do this, the gas is moved through a compressor into thinner coils on the outside of the unit. This puts it under pressure. When the gas is put under pressure it warms and returns to its liquid state. The liquid inside is warmer than room temperature so the heat is transferred from the coils to the room. So, if you put heat into the front of the fridge, it ends up coming out the back.

The cool air in the front of the refrigerator is balanced by the heat radiating from the back.

Therefore, instead of producing net work, as a heat engine does, it would require an input of work. A general term for this type of machine is a heat pump. Refrigerators and air conditioners are two kinds of heat pumps.

In designing heat engines, we want to maximize the temperature differences of the reservoirs to operate at the highest efficiency possible. A heat pump is a different matter. A large difference in temperature between the reservoirs means that a large amount of energy is required to operate the heat pump. It is more desirable that a heat pump minimize the temperature difference between reservoirs and use a minimal amount of energy. Engineers try to design "energy efficient" refrigerators that do not use much electricity.

The effectiveness of a heat pump is described as the "coefficient of performance," or the C.O.P. Just as there is an equation for the ideal Carnot efficiency, there is an equation for the C.O.P. of the ideal reversible heat pump:

$$C.O.P. = \frac{TL}{TH-TL}$$

T is measured in Kelvin.

If you compare the equations, you will see that both depend on the difference between temperatures of the two reservoirs. The Carnot efficiency increases as the temperature difference increases. The opposite occurs for the C.O.P. The effectiveness of the heat pump decreases as the temperature difference increases.

In practical terms, when it's really hot outside, your air conditioner becomes less efficient and uses a lot more electricity to get your house to your desired temperature.

Energy bills can be hair-raising when temperatures rise.

Hot to Cold

Toasting marshmallows requires very
little of the heat generated by a fire.

FOUR

A Matter of Time

Time machines have long caught our imagination, but the second law of thermodynamics says they can't exist. This is because of entropy, which requires one direction of time, sometimes called the "Arrow of Time."

Simply put, wood doesn't unburn, exhaust from a car can't be reformed into gas, and energy moves from concentrated to less concentrated forms. When we burn coal, some of the heat is discarded and can't be recovered. Therefore, the world as we know it can never be restored to the way it was, so we can't turn back the clock.

Clausius coined the term "entropy," defining it in terms of heat and temperature. Entropy is a property of matter, since it can be measured, but it is not something we can see or touch.

The word "heat" has a more specific meaning in thermodynamic terms than in everyday usage. When we speak of "heat" in our daily lives, we might mean either warmth or temperature—not necessarily the scientific definition of a transfer

A gas fire heats a pan, which in turn heats the kitchen.

of energy from a higher to a lower temperature. In the same way, entropy has taken on a meaning other than its original one in thermodynamics. "Entropy" is sometimes used synonymously with "chaos" or "disorder." In thermodynamics, entropy always refers to the measure of the dispersal of energy, at a certain temperature.

A pan heated will disperse heat throughout the kitchen. Entropy measures the dispersal of that energy as it moves outward from a concentrated area. Entropy originates in the microscopic arrangement of matter, which exists as solids, liquids, or gases. Matter is made up of atoms, usually combined with other atoms to form clusters called molecules. Molecules are in constant motion, colliding with each other and changing direction. Nineteenth-century scientists compared the motion of gas molecules to a game of billiards, with one ball ricocheting off another. In this analogy, every ball is constantly in motion, moving at very high speeds. Gas molecules ricocheting off each other in space are unlikely to spontaneously form an orderly arrangement.

Understanding the Laws *of* Thermodynamics

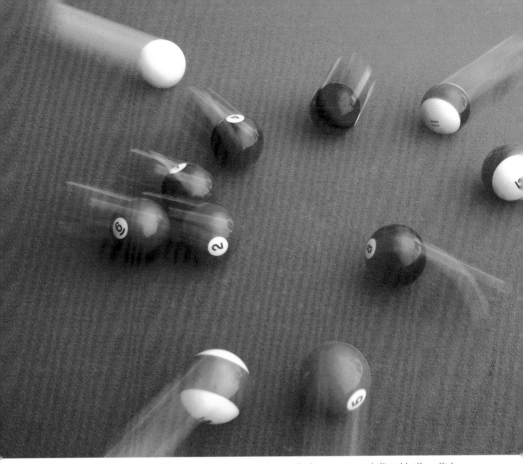

Heated molecules collide in a closed system in much the same way billiard balls collide immediately after a break.

What does this have to do with entropy, as defined as the measure of the dispersal of energy? As molecules collide, they exchange energy. Unless it is in an isolated system, an object exchanges energy with the surroundings as well as with other molecules within the system. If the object is heated, such as our pan, its energy increases. The molecules that make up the pan begin to move more rapidly. They disperse this extra energy from heat to the molecules in their surroundings, which are moving more slowly. Overall entropy increases during the process.

A change in entropy can occur without a change in temperature. Phase changes are the transition from one state of matter to another. Molecules in solids are tightly held in a rigid configuration and can move only slightly. Molecules in liquids

Road to
Solar Power

Earth receives only one two-billionths of the energy output of the
sun, but according to the National Geographic Society and other
environmental groups, the sun shines enough energy on our planet
in one hour to meet the needs of the planet for one year.

The key is finding ways of harnessing some of that energy. In
2014, only two percent of the electricity generated in the United
States came from solar power. Much of this is generated in remote
locations, which means the electricity has to travel a great distance to
be used. The energy degrades the farther it travels.

Photovoltaic panels that people put on their homes generate
power that can be stored and used right away, so less will be lost
to degradation. However, these panels are inefficient, capturing
only 10 to 20 percent of the light that strikes them. Developing
nanotechnology can increase efficiency and lower costs for
photovoltaic cells. So far, researchers into this technology have been
able to capture about 70 percent of the available energy.

George Brusaw of Idaho wants to pave our 28,000 square miles
(72,000 square kilometers) of roads with heavy glass panels so our
roadways can be used as solar power collectors. He claims this could
meet all of our energy needs. The electricity could power heating
coils to melt snow and ice, making roads safer. An electrical engineer,
Brusaw and his wife, Julie, installed a parking pad at their home in
Idaho. It remained snow free during the winter of 2013–2014.

There are still hurdles to be cleared, but this idea could pave the
way to widescale use of green energy.

can move more freely, but they still interact with each other. Gas molecules move freely and tend to diffuse. During phase changes, entropy changes even though the temperature remains constant.

Entropy tends to increase in any case that molecules can freely move to disperse themselves throughout a larger area.

ENERGY BECOMES LESS USEFUL

According to the second law of thermodynamics, work can be completely transformed into heat, but the reverse can never be true. Some heat will always be discarded in the transformation of heat to work. For this reason, the second law is sometimes called the law of degradation of energy.

Energy dumped into the low temperature reservoir of a heat engine can be described as lower quality than energy in the high temperature reservoir. Since it is less useful for doing work, the quality of the energy in the low temperature reservoir has been degraded. For processes involving heat transfer, the amount of energy available for doing work decreases.

At the same time, entropy increases during heat transfers. These two tendencies can be taken together: as entropy increases, energy is constantly being degraded and stored at lower temperatures. Natural processes tend to generate entropy and diminish the quality of energy.

THE THIRD LAW OF THERMODYNAMICS

The third law of thermodynamics addresses a practical aspect of entropy. We know that if a beaker of water is heated, its entropy increases. Scientists can measure the entropy change in a lab. Measuring the change in entropy tells us only about the difference in entropy between the initial and the final state. This measurement is relative. It conveys nothing about the **absolute** entropy of the beaker of water at a specific temperature.

In 1906, a German chemist named Walther Nernst presented the Nernst heat theorem. This law is often referred to as the third

Walther Nernst helped formulate the third law of thermodynamics.

law of thermodynamics. It states that at absolute zero, a perfectly crystalline substance has zero entropy.

Absolute zero is the lowest theoretical temperature possible, representing a complete absence of heat. It is equal to zero on the Kelvin temperature scale, −273.15°C, or −459.67°F. Absolute zero cannot be achieved in a finite number of steps. In other words, no matter how cold something is, it can always be made colder without ever reaching absolute zero. Lab experiments studying the behavior of matter at absolute zero can only be performed at temperatures near absolute zero. At absolute zero, molecular motion comes to a standstill. There are no energy interactions between molecules and zero entropy.

If there is zero entropy, that means there would be no change, so you could go back in time. However, because life as we know it would no longer exist at absolute zero, there doesn't seem to be a lot of future in it.

Nonetheless, scientists have made great strides in creating more efficient engines and ways to create and use energy. It's all thanks to what they understand about the laws of thermodynamics.

GLOSSARY

absolute Independent of arbitrary standards of measurement.

beaker A type of laboratory glassware consisting of a cylindrical cup with a notch on the top to allow for the pouring of liquids.

boundary The line or plane indicating the limit or extent of something.

British thermal unit (BTU) A unit of heat equal to the amount of heat needed to raise one pound of water 1°F (−17.22°C).

calorie The quantity of heat required to raise the temperature of one gram of water by 1°C (1.8°F).

displacement The act of physically moving something to another position.

electromagnet A temporary magnet made by coiling wire around an iron core. When current flows in the coil, the iron becomes a magnet.

finite The state of having fixed limits or bounds.

foot-pound A unit of work equal to a force of one pound moving through a distance of one foot.

force The push or pull upon an object, causing displacement, resulting from the object's interaction with another object.

heat The transferal of energy across the boundary of a system (or the surroundings) to another system at a lower temperature because of a difference in temperature between the two systems.

insulator An object designed to prevent the loss of heat or electricity.

joule A unit of energy used to calculate the amount of work done within a certain space.

monograph A scholarly book, article, or pamphlet on a specialized subject.

system In thermodynamics, the part of the universe of interest or under scrutiny.

thermal equilibrium The point at which energy gained by a system
is balanced by the energy lost.

thermodynamics The study of energy transfers and transformations.

work The energy required to move an object against an opposing force.

FURTHER INFORMATION

BOOKS

Atkins, Peter. *The Laws of Thermodynamics: A Very Short Introduction*. Oxford, United Kingdom: Oxford University Press, 2010.

Pauken, Mike. *Thermodynamics for Dummies*. Hoboken, NJ: John Wiley & Sons, 2011.

Van Ness, H.C. *Understanding Thermodynamics*. Mineola, NY: Dover Publications, 1983.

WEBSITES

National Aeronautics and Space Administration
www.grc.nasa.gov/WWW/k-12/airplane/thermo.html

Our national scientists walk you through concepts in thermodynamics and other subjects in this site featuring text and video links.

The Physics Classroom
www.physicsclassroom.com

This comprehensive tutorial provides instruction for beginning physics students, and is an outstanding resource for their teachers.

PhysLink.com
www.physlink.com

The Physics and Astronomy Online Journal provides news and educational resources.

BIBLIOGRAPHY

Atkins, P. W. *The Second Law*. New York, NY: Scientific American Library, 1984.

Craig, Norman C. *Entropy Analysis: An Introduction to Chemical Thermodynamics*. New York, NY: VCH Publishers, Inc., 1992.

Fenn, John B. *Engines, Energy, and Entropy: A Thermodynamics Primer*. San Francisco, CA: W. H. Freeman and Company, 1982.

Goldstein, Martin, and Inge F. Goldstein. *The Refrigerator and the Universe: Understanding the Laws of Energy*. Cambridge, MA: Harvard University Press, 1993.

Kondepudi, Dilip, and Ilya Prigogine. *Modern Thermodynamics: From Heat Engines to Dissipative Structures*. New York, NY: John Wiley & Sons, Inc., 1998.

Lambert, Frank. "Entropy Sites—A Guide." April 2004. Retrieved May 11, 2004, www.entropysite.com.

Van Wylen, Gordon J., and Richard E. Sonntag. *Fundamentals of Classical Thermodynamics*. New York, NY: John Wiley & Sons, Inc., 1965.

Von Baeyer, Hans Christian. *Maxwell's Demon: Why Warmth Disperses and Time Passes*. New York, NY: Random House, 1998.

INDEX